# WHAT THE F**K ARE THE THREE PRINCIPLES?

---

## And 18 Other Questions Answered From So-called Wisdom

Amir Karkouti

WHAT THE F**K ARE THE THREE PRINCIPLES?
And 18 Other Questions Answered
From So-called Wisdom

ISBN-13: 978-0-692-06356-9

Printed in the United States of America

First Printing, 2018

# Table of Contents

■ ■ ■

*Never obey anyone's command unless it's coming from within you also.*

Osho

# Author's Note

*A few thoughts...about Thought.*

In this book, you will notice that the word "thought" is sometimes capitalized and sometimes appears in lowercase. This is intentional. I can tell you with 100% certainty that my editor was not intoxicated when she was editing my book.

When I am speaking about Thought, I am describing the formless energy behind every experience. The energy of Thought is neutral.

Lowercase thought describes the personal thinking we have. This is personal to us.

Everyone reading this is using the energy of Thought. You have to have a mechanism for your senses to make sense of the world. However, everyone who reads this book will have a different experience of what they are reading; that is lowercase thought. In other words, no two people will see the world the same (thought), even though they are using the same energy to create it (Thought).

Please keep this in mind as you read this book.

■ ■ ■

# Short Intro

You're probably wondering whether you've picked up the wrong book. Isn't this supposed to be a spiritual book about the discovery of the Three Principles by a man named Sydney Banks? Well, it is. The thing is, I was never really good at being "enlightened." I was just good at being me and stumbling across things. Luckily, I stumbled across the Principles before I heard the terrible news I will share in the next chapter.

Of course, you don't have to spend time reading this snippet of my journey around the Three Principles. However, if you want to entertain the idea of seeing the power of the Principles in action in the form of a not-so-kosher story, grab yourself some popcorn and enjoy the ride.

You can jump to the Q & A section after the first chapter and get right to the main section of the book. The questions in this book came from all of the amazing people in my Facebook group, which is called "What the F*#K Are the Principles." Some of the questions will overlap, and that's OK — you might hear something the second time that you missed the first go-around.

Now, of course, the answers in this book will most likely change. But from what I see at this moment in time, these are the best answers I can offer.

**What will not change** are the Principles of Universal Mind, Universal Thought, and Universal Consciousness. There are plenty of books that define these terms, so I won't beat the spiritual unicorn to give you my take on what they are. I'm assuming you've been around the Principles, or at least know enough about them, to know what those terms mean. If you don't, I have provided a list of videos, audio material, and lectures by Sydney Banks at the end of the book.

Now, on with the show...

*You are as close to Truth right this second as you ever will be. Why don't you just learn to relax and appreciate what you have in life? When you do, I guarantee that you'll stand a far greater chance of finding what you are looking for than by running all over the world looking for it.*

Syd Banks

# The 3P's
# The Principles, Propecia, and My Penis

*Life goes on, unconcerned whether*
*interpretation is present or absent.*
Vijai S. Shankar

I never thought I'd have the type of freedom I got the day I discovered that my penis might never work again.

I remember the day so vividly. My wife was sitting on my right, and the prestigious Editor-in-Chief of *The Journal of Sexual Medicine,* world-famous urologist Dr. Irwin Goldstein, was sitting in front of me with all his certificates and degrees plastered on the wall behind him.

Dr. Goldstein is a straight shooter and got right down to business. The whole thing was fascinating from the outset. He was looking at my blood results and making faces as if he were inspecting a diamond. Finally, he looked up after what felt like forever and asked a simple question: "Have you ever taken Propecia, Amir?"

I casually stated, "Oh, yeah, I took it for about six years but my wife got me to quit after she read that she could make deformed babies if she merely touched a pill."

Turns out, I had innocently taken a pill that my

general practitioner told me would reduce hair loss. I didn't think I was taking anything that could destroy my endocrine system.

What happened next only happens in movies...or to be precise, in horror films.

Dr. Goldstein slammed his fist on his desk and screamed out in his least professional voice, "FUCK!"

His whole desk shook and all the little medical trinkets and pens jumped as much as we did.

My wife and I waited patiently for him to hopefully say, "Just kidding, you're gonna be fine..."

But he didn't. Instead, he went on to say, "By your bloodwork, I knew something was up. Based on your hormone levels and your symptoms, you are a classic case of somebody who has 'crashed' from taking Finasteride, the generic version of Propecia. What this means is that I can probably fix all the stuff you're experiencing, like mental fatigue, muscle wasting, memory loss, anxiety, physical exhaustion, and so on. However, the last thing that tends to improve is erectile function. In other words, your penis might never work again. Amir, you are a classic case of what's called Post-Finasteride Syndrome."

My immediate response was, "Great, Doc! At least I know what's wrong."

As happy as I was to hear that what I was experiencing could actually be diagnosed, a wave hit me right afterward that dissolved my momentary relief. I had thoughts about having children with my wife.

How was that going to work out? I had thoughts about why a doctor would prescribe this shit to men, and darker thoughts of suing the disgusting pharmaceutical company for damaging a young man such as myself, and the thousands of other men who were probably going through this as well.

But here's where it got interesting.

I could see myriad thoughts passing by, and each of them had an emotion tied to it. I was literally in a maze of thought-feelings, going from feeling blessed to feeling like shit and back again.

At that moment, I realized something. The circumstance had nothing to do with the thoughts that entered my mind. In other words, the doctor told me a situation that had happened, and within five minutes I jumped onto a ride of emotions. No feeling had more validity than another. I couldn't pinpoint which emotion was truly tied to what the doctor had said.

Dr. Goldstein kept talking, and it started to sound like Kermit the Frog. He was going on about the treatment protocol, and it literally sounded like, "BLAH BLAH BLAH..." to me.

I was finally at peace.

I knew Dr. Goldstein had told me something that I "should" have felt bad about...but I didn't. Granted, bad feelings came and went, but so did good ones. And behind all that was racing through my mind, I saw the capacity I had to have *any* thought, at *any* moment, about *any* situation. I was free to experience thought taking form, moment by moment. And thought DID take form, regardless of what I was told. He could have said that I had peanut butter and jelly in my blood-work, and I could have been angry, sad, jealous, excited (enter feeling here) or whatever Universal Thought was offering me. I saw it for the very first time. *Thought* was not related to the *circumstance*. The energy of Thought can show up with anything, and I will, by design, feel that thought.

I saw the gift in action right before my eyes. I was in Heaven on Earth — not because of what the doctor said, but because I had a deeper feeling for who we are that was independent of what I had just heard.

My wife popped me out of this feeling of bliss when the doctor tried to get my attention. I think I came back to Earth about the third time the doctor said my name.

"Amir…hey, Amir, are you OK? You seem a bit calm after the news I just sprang on you."

I was still coming down from the high when my wife gently grabbed my knee and gave it a pat, and said, "Oh, Doc, I think Amir is too naïve to see this as a problem right now."

I knew what she meant. Maybe she got a glimpse too. Who knows? I never asked. But what I heard when she said this was that I didn't see it as a *problem* at all. I saw it as a *circumstance*. I knew that, regardless of what the doctor said, the energy of Thought would make it seem like my feelings around what I had heard were coming from the doctor...but I *saw* it with my own eyes. I saw the different thoughts and feelings that passed through with the news. I didn't connect the circumstance with the feeling. Had I given it more thought than it needed, I would have believed that the *circumstance* made me feel the distress, anger, and frustration associated with the news I'd just received. We will always experience an infinite level of feelings, no matter what circumstances arise. But for some reason, I knew at that moment that no feeling can ever be tied to a circumstance; it can only be tied to the *thinking* that shows up in the moment *in spite of* the circumstance.

What I was experiencing wasn't simply the fact that my ding-a-ling might not work; I was feeling Thought flow through me, which was giving me the *experience* that I was angry at the circumstance. I was experiencing the energy of Thought taking form, independent of my circumstances. I thought about this for a minute. If I had been under anesthesia when the doc told me the news, I wouldn't have cared. I wouldn't have cared because there wouldn't be any *thought* to give it the experience. I need the *energy* of Thought to experience the situation as good, bad, ugly, or terrifying. That was so surreal!

And as strange as this may sound, I wouldn't trade the experience and "secret" I discovered during this brief encounter with my doctor for anything! OK fine, maybe I'd rather have had this experience getting ice cream or being gifted a new Tesla, but I'll take what I can get.

And what I got was the Principles in action. What I got is what Sydney Banks so eloquently spoke about in his books and lectures. Strange as it may seem, I became a new man even though I lost a part of my manhood. I guess many men might never understand this, but it's possible.

I now volunteer for Dr. Goldstein and speak to several patients a week who tell me that they are broken (or at least they think they are), that erectile dysfunction has ruined their lives and they will never be the same. I know one thing for sure: What I experienced is the Truth of our reality. It only works one way — from the inside out. So, having truth on my side helps when I speak to these men, who innocently believe that this circumstance has ruined them. I know that's impossible because as long as they have the capacity for fresh, new thought, the thought of them being ruined is just as fleeting as them seeing that they are *not* ruined.

Alan Watts once said, "You are not obligated to be the same person you were five minutes ago." I would upgrade the quote to, "You are not obligated to believe the thought you had a moment ago."

As long as you see your capacity, your God-given right to the Gift of Thought, moment to moment, then you are free from all circumstances. You are free from the shackles of the ups and downs of the energy of

Thought. We are free to go beyond personal thinking, which can't influence our true nature behind thought.

You are beyond all of it. You are not only beyond it, *you are it!* You are the source from which all of it comes into creation.

We forget that.

I think we were designed to forget...

After all, what fun would it be to always know our gifts? Then we wouldn't have human moments like this to write about. So, we get glimpses of what we are capable of. We get glimpses that our reality is made of Thought, yet Thought itself is not made of reality.

We are the vessel that creation comes from. When you see it that way, there is no way that life can't be beautiful.

I just wish somebody had told me this earlier.

# WHAT THE F**K ARE THE THREE PRINCIPLES?
## and Other Questions

I will do the best I can to answer the questions in this book based on the way I see things. But don't take my word for it. As a matter of fact, your own responses may be better for you because they come from you. However, I wanted to respond to these as a way of reflection. The answers are not set in stone. They are more like writings on water...the writing will change form as it enters your world, and hopefully, you will see something new.

One of my favorite authors, Osho, has a commandment that fits here nicely: "Never obey anyone's command unless it is coming from within you also."

If you arrive at a different answer than I have, I won't be offended — I'd be delighted! Feel free to see what shows up for you as you look into my answers. I will try to respond to these questions in the most human way possible. What that means is, you won't hear me getting my angel wings out and speaking to you in a soft, harmonic voice. There is a reason for that...because this stuff needs to be heard from "our" level. No fluff, no guru stuff, no Cocoa Puffs. (That made no sense at all...I just wanted it to rhyme and sound good.)

OK, back to what I was saying. Hopefully, the

answers will strike a dialogue with your gentle boss called Wisdom. Wisdom shows up in crazy places. Hopefully, my responses will either bring forth your wisdom or piss her off enough to say, "Don't listen to Amir…he doesn't know what he's talking about!"

Whatever she decides to say…follow her. She probably knows more than I do.

All right, I'm going to stop stalling now and get to the questions. Again, I want to give heartfelt thanks to everyone who participated in bringing this book to life. I also want to thank all of my teachers, practitioners, and colleagues who helped me and put up with me along the way. Thanks for your patience and love.

*Mind, Consciousness, and Thought are the Three Principles that enable us to acknowledge and respond to existence.*

*They are the basic building blocks, and it is through these three components that all psychological mysteries are unfolded.*

Syd Banks

# — Question #1 —

## What are the Three Principles?

Screw it, I lied. I was tempted not to write anything about what the Three Principles are, but I know eventually some newbie will pick up this book and say, "How the heck is he going to write about the Three Principles and not tell us what they are?" So, I'll make my best attempt to explain the Three Principles.

First, I have to hand the mike to Sydney Banks; the person who practically came up with these Principles. He didn't actually come up with them, but he put together what all the other spiritual teachers have known for years and created something cohesive and so easy to understand that even an idiot like me could grasp it.

In Syd's own way of stating what the Three Principles are, he wrote:

> Mind, Consciousness, and Thought are spiritual gifts that enable us to see creation and guide us through life. All three are universal constants that can never change or never be separated. All psychological functions are born of these three principles." (Page 22, *The Missing Link* by Sydney Banks)

What the heck does that mean?

Let's start with Principle #1: **Universal Mind.** Universal Mind runs the show. While my wife was pregnant and eating ice cream mixed with cereal, her body used that yummy combo and turned it into food that allowed a baby to grow in her belly. I am no scientist, but that shit was crazy! She could literally eat anything and that turned into something nutritious in her body to feed a life immersed in fluid. As much as I'd love to give her credit for doing that…something else was doing the "hard" work. She just had to shove food in her mouth! (Don't tell her I said that. As far as she knows, she did all the work.)

That's Universal Mind at play. It's the part of the Universe that keeps ticking, creating, and growing in order for life to sustain itself. Check this out: Half of your lungs are hanging on a tree! You cannot survive without trees because they convert carbon dioxide into the oxygen you breathe. The carbon dioxide you are exhaling comes from the carbon that you eat! The carbon dioxide is dissolved in your blood, carried to your lungs via circulation, and you breathe it out. As you are reading this, you are doing a billion things that are keeping you alive. But it's not you doing "it"…is it? You would screw it up because really, you aren't that smart to operate this machinery and you know it.

### THAT'S UNIVERSAL MIND, BABY!!!

OK, I just got super excited because when I think about how amazing this is, it still blows me away. And that's just one Principle. The Principle of Universal Mind is also known as the Invisible Life Force, Chi, Baraka, Amir Karkouti, the Holy Spirit, Yahweh, Vital Energy, God...you get it. Everyone has heard of this life force. And if you are a scientist and this concept of Universal Mind is too woo-woo for you, know this: It's the "thing" that allows the Universe to be constant enough for us to study it. The fact that life is consistent enough for it to be measured, and the fact that nature is always consistent, is what we call Natural Law. And that's what we are talking about!

Now, on to Principle #2: **Universal Thought.** Universal Thought is when this invisible energy takes form and gives us our moment-to-moment experience. It's not the personal thought we are used to hearing. Here's how I explain it in my recovery groups.

Each and every one of you in my group is sitting here and thinking about something. Some of you are thinking about lunch. Others want to leave and go to the beach. Some of you are wondering why the guy who is talking about thought is so handsome. That's beside the point. The point is that all of you have the capacity for Thought and each of you has been gifted to bring Thought into form, moment to moment. In other words, bring 100 people into this room and you will have 100 different thoughts. However, each person in this room is using the same capacity to bring forth whatever thought arises in each moment, and that's the Principle of Thought. The Principle of Thought is neutral; it is energy that allows personal thoughts to have feelings and aliveness. Where are the thoughts coming from? Where were they before you had them? I'm not sure. All I know is that Thought is the invisible energy that takes form and allows each of us to experience what we experience. As Syd Banks once said, "Thought is not reality; yet it is through Thought that realities are created."

The same space that created the capacity for energy to take form to have you think you are a lowlife loser is the same energy that will magically take another form and have you wondering what color you should paint your nails. Once you see that, you'll start to discover that the thought that tells you that you are worthless is made from the same material as the thought that tells you the best nail color to try with your new outfit. But until you see it, one will appear to be more important than the other. However, when you do see it, you will notice that both are neutral and no more "real" than the next thought that will take form in any given moment.

This gives you the freedom to know that all thoughts are neutral by nature. Some "appear" more solid, more real, and newsworthy; however, they are made from the exact material as all the other thoughts you will have today. They are all created by Universal Thought taking form in consciousness, moment to moment.

Principle #3 is **Universal Consciousness.** You cannot have a thought take form unless a thought connects to consciousness. Consciousness brings our thinking to life through all of our senses. Don't believe me? I wonder how much that devastating thought you're having right now is worth if I put you under anesthesia? Oh, you're not conscious enough to worry about that fight between you and your wife when the anesthesiologist has gotten ahold of you. Yeah, I thought so! You need consciousness for a thought to take form and for you to experience it.

As Syd Banks said, "Consciousness allows the recognition of form, form being the expression of thought."

The Three Principles of Mind, Consciousness, and Thought are the building blocks required in order to experience life. If one is missing, the whole thing breaks down. In Christianity, they have the Trinity. It turns out that there is a Trinity that explains all of psychology as well. It's these Three Universal Principles that, once they are understood, give us the psychological freedom we all yearn to find.

If that didn't make sense, go email this dude by the name of Michael Neill...he'll probably give you a better answer.

*All you have to know is everything is created from Thought, you don't have to know anything else.*

Syd Banks

## — Question #2 —

## How do I distinguish which thoughts to trust? In other words, how can I tell the difference between wisdom and just more thought?

Great question, but the answers are always in the question. If you are asking the question, you probably have doubts about its worthiness. I don't mean to be crass, but that's kind of like asking, "Do I need to poop right now?" If you're asking yourself, then you probably don't have to poop. The body will let us know physically when it needs to do what it needs to do. It's spontaneous. Our wisdom, which is harder to see because it's invisible, tells us in its spontaneity as well. When we are in flow, we don't ask, we just *do*. We call it our "gut feeling," the little voice of clarity or wisdom within us. So, don't worry about which thoughts to trust. By the time you've followed your wisdom, the question won't make sense. And if you're still wondering whether that's wisdom, you're probably not in wisdom.

The good news is, when you don't concern yourself with the question any further, the answer tends to show up. It's a cat-and-mouse game, but we are both the cat and the mouse. Wondering which thoughts to trust will matter less and less. Our inner wisdom will give us an answer before our intellect tries to grapple with it. Wisdom *feels* different. Wisdom has a peaceful feeling. As Syd would say, "Follow the feeling." Relax. Something new is bound to appear.

*Sydney Banks' tremendous gift to the world was to bring simple principles along that would help people understand what Buddha was talking about, what Jesus was talking about—everyone!—Maslow, Carl Rogers and William James. The Principles, if you look at them deeply, are behind what everyone is talking about. Everyone is saying that Thought is what creates your reality, and that we are all a part of something much, much greater.*

Ami Chen Mill-Naim

# — Question #3 —

## What is the difference between the Three Principles and the things the sages of the ages have said? Seems like Buddha and Jesus were saying similar things.

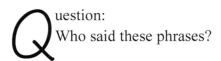

uestion:
Who said these phrases?

A) "It is the thought-life that pollutes. For it is from within, out of a person's heart, that evil thoughts come — sexual immorality, theft, murder, adultery, greed, malice, deceit, lewdness, envy, slander, arrogance and folly. All these evils come from inside and defile a person."

B) "We are shaped by our thoughts; we become what we think. When the mind is pure, joy follows like a shadow that never leaves."

C) "The misled thoughts of humanity, alienated from their inner wisdom, cause all violence, cruelty, and savagery in this world."

D) "A great silence overcomes me, and I wonder why I ever thought to use language."

E) "To be fearless isn't to really overcome fear, it's to come to know its nature."

F) "We're fascinated by the words — but where we meet is in the silence behind them."

Can you tell me which one is Buddha, Jesus, Rumi, Ram Dass, Pema Chodron, or Sydney Banks? Probably not. Even when I went back to edit the quotes, I still couldn't put the person with the quote. These were some powerful people, who, like Syd Banks, have tapped into their divine intelligence. Can you guess which one is Syd Banks and which ones aren't?

All right, I'll give you the answers here:

A) Jesus (Mark 7:20, *The Living Bible*)
B) Buddha
C) Sydney Banks (*The Missing Link*, page 84)
D) Rumi
E) Pema Chodron (*Start From Where You Are*)
F) Ram Dass

So yes, Jesus, Buddha, Sydney, and all the spiritual greats had similar things to say about the nature of thought. I had to throw a wrench in there and put Pema Chodron and Ram Dass in the mix to show that even living spiritual teachers have something to say about this ageless wisdom. I am sure all of us can find thousands of quotes that have a similar tone; enough to fill a whole library.

One of the great storytellers and philosophers of our time, Martin Buber, said:

I stand in a chain of narrators, a link between links; I tell once again the old stories, and if they sound new, it is because the new already lay dormant in them when they were told the first time.

Even with Buber (not to be confused with Justin Bieber, the other great philosopher of our time), he saw that the sages had similar wisdom to share. So, what makes Sydney Banks different? What was it about his wisdom that should be separated out from the others?

I'll speak for myself. When I heard Syd, there was something about the simplicity of what he was sharing that allowed me to see that I had the same wisdom. For the first time, I got that he wasn't speaking as a sage. He was telling us in plain language that the same wisdom he is sharing is the same wisdom we have hidden behind our veil of personal thinking.

As I mentioned before, all the other great sages were saying this, but I always felt that they were just bright individuals, and maybe, in a few lifetimes, I'd get to their level of brilliance. Something about Syd changed all that. I won't say that I'm a Rumi or Jesus, but I was able to share what I saw in my own way and people started to hear it. I think it's because Syd not only shared his wisdom, he came forth with a set of Principles that govern all of our psychology. The other sages knew how wisdom worked, but Syd showed us that wisdom, and all of reality, can be discovered through the governing Principles of Mind, Consciousness, and Thought. He was able to trace back where all the truths were flowing from. Interestingly enough, after reading Syd's work, I could go back and connect to the other sages at a deeper level.

Syd's teachings were also not derivatives of passed-down wisdom and knowledge. He allowed me, and many others who have been struck by his teachings, to see that we have the availability of wisdom at any moment. As long as we have the capacity for fresh, new thought, wisdom is only one thought away. I was able to see the freshness of a new thought that gave me real-time wisdom when I needed it.

Another thing that struck me about Syd's teachings is that he continually goes back to the source of our experience. Pick up the book *The Missing Link* and you'll see that he talks about Mind, Consciousness, and Thought as Three Spiritual Truths of all life, over and over again. Many sages veer off and talk about the implications of what happens when you see a deeper truth. Syd, on the other hand, points to the source and allows the reader to see the implications. In other words, once I saw the source of our experience by the Gift of Mind, brought to life by Consciousness, created in Thought, I was able to see right through to the core of all life.

Syd Banks was adamant not to make these Truths a prescription. Unlike many teachings, there isn't a "therefore" after what he says. In other words, you don't have to go to church and play bingo on Tuesday nights if you don't want to. You don't have to pray in a certain direction unless it's something you enjoy.

In 1875, Mary Baker Eddy wrote a book called *Science and Health,* and it's packed with wisdom. I purchased this book to humor myself one day. I recently opened it to a few pages, and damn! There are some incredible quotes in there that blew my mind! In Chapter 4 of her book she writes, "Evil has no reality. It is neither person, place, nor thing, but simply a belief, an illusion of material sense."

Tell me that doesn't sound like the 3P's! That could have been said by Syd while he was sipping tea. The difference, however, is that Mary Baker Eddy goes on to give prescriptions for how to get closer to God and live a healthy life via the scriptures. Syd, on the other hand, believed that your wisdom is enough to steer you in the right direction. The Three Principles have no formula, no prescription, nothing to follow but your own wisdom. His teachings didn't conflict with any religious, humanist, or psychological schools of thought. He pointed to life before it took form. That was his entire message.

When I shared the Principles to the best of my ability, other people got glimpses of this deeper truth. I felt like I had a spiritual guru pop out of my mind and say shit that I couldn't have come up with on my own. It's not that it's magical, it's that when you can see the truth of our nature, magical stuff tends to happen. Kind of like the story about when the doctor told me about my erectile dysfunction. I saw the truth of what was going on in the moment, which allowed me to transcend the experience beyond the personal roller-coaster ride of thought.

And, of course, as soon as I thought I "got" how the universe worked, and somebody asked me what I said that sparked an insight, I'd forget again because I was using my intellect instead of wisdom in the moment to come up with a clever answer. That's when I've heard of Syd telling people who got into their heads to, "Go home!"

A couple more things I see that differentiate Syd from other teachers. As I mentioned before, Syd was interested in the principles of how our psychology worked. He saw that our lives are created moment by moment by the Spiritual Energy of Thought taking form. That gives us total freedom to have any feeling show up at any time. That did something for me. I would read things by Alan Watts and totally get it, until I had a shitty day. All of a sudden, I'd ask myself, "If I get it, then why do I feel like shit?" When I see that my thoughts are transient by nature, and my personal experience of life will change moment by moment, I can clearly see that I am OK, regardless of whether I feel like shit. And that is a gift!

Syd gave us the logic behind how our thoughts create our reality. Syd didn't say that thoughts have a big part in it, Syd said IT'S ALL THOUGHT!

## ALL THOUGHT!

Not 99% thought and 1% chocolate (although that would have made my day). His gift was that he was diligent — almost militant — not to stray away from these Principles. Finally, he allowed idiots like me to be able to grasp this wisdom somehow. He enabled me to see the wisdom in everyone. He enabled me to understand why somebody would believe that their circumstance is causing their stress, worry, anxiety, or happiness. He also allowed me to see that it can never come from outside of us. Life, as we experience it, always takes form in Thought and comes to life in Consciousness. He allowed me to be OK with the illusion that sometimes it feels like life is happening from the outside in because of our circumstances. He saw that, eventually, we'd pop back into our wisdom and see that it's all happening from the inside out via the energy of Thought in the moment.

Do you want to know why it took me so long to see this? Because my dumb ass continually compared Syd to all the other great sages. Every time his name showed up, I would say, "Oh, that's like what Rumi said," or "Yeah, Jesus said that too, then he washed somebody's stanky feet."

The problem was, I was going back to what I already knew with the hope of hearing something different. In other words, I wasn't hearing anything new because I was too busy comparing it with something from the past. Syd was adamant about telling us to stop looking where we have already looked. The wisdom will come from the unknown, where you haven't looked. Even when he said that in his writings, I would say, "Oh, that's clever...go look into the unknown. I know how to do that, I just read about the unknown in another book...so I've got that one covered."

That doesn't look like the unknown to me. That looks like somebody who didn't shut up because he thought he knew it all already!

If you are new to his writings or haven't discovered what is different about what Syd is saying, stop reading this book right now! I'm serious...STOP, and go read a Syd Banks book with fresh eyes. Go see what he is saying from a new place, then come back and tell me if you see something new. I assure you that if you get a glimpse of what he is trying to express, your world will change. The funny part is, it won't be because of anything that you read. It will be you stepping into the unknown with a teacher who has been there and who will break what we experience down to its simplest form.

What is its simplest form? It's that all of reality is created by these Three Gifts or Universal Principles: **The Principles of Universal Mind, Universal Consciousness, and Universal Thought.**

OK, now go read his books or listen to one of his CDs, even if it's your second or third time around, to get a better understanding of those Principles. And if you get overloaded and start overthinking the Principles, chill out and go home!

*The solutions to outwardly complex problems
created by misguided thoughts will not arise from
complicated analytical theory, but will emerge as an
insight, wrapped in a blanket of simplicity.*

Syd Banks

# — Question #4 —

## How do I get out of an intellectual understanding of the Three Principles?

*O*K, first you have to crack two eggs and whisk them. Be careful not to get any eggshells in the pan. After gently whisking the eggs, please touch your heart chakra and chant:

NO MORE INTELLECT!
NO MORE INTELLECT!
NO MORE INTELLECT!
JUST EGGS!

If that doesn't do the trick...

Shit. I have nothing else to offer you. Well, OK, I kinda have something else to offer. Let's unpack this for a minute.

I, as a male living in the United States, have an average life span of 78 years before I croak. Seventy-eight years broken down into minutes is 40,996,800 minutes, give or take, that I will enjoy on this Earth.

Let's say you intellectually think about the Three Principles every day for 60 minutes a day. In my lifetime I would have used 1,708,200 minutes to think about the Principles out of the 40,996,800 minutes I have here on Earth. In other words, who cares? What's the problem?

I'll tell you what the problem is. It's that we think it's a problem that we have intellectual ideas and thoughts around things that we aren't supposed to. And it's in the "supposed to" that we feel like we are not doing the Spiritual Journey correctly.

Instead of wondering how to get out of the intellectual understanding of the Principles, what if that was part of the trip? What if God or Syd or whoever showed up on TV and said, "Ladies and gentlemen, follow your heart and feel the feeling beyond the intellect. However, please allow 1,708,200 minutes of the journey for some intellectual scrambling. Some of you might use more of those minutes and some of you might use less. However, you are designed to go in and out of intellectual thought and drop into your spiritual essence. Enjoy both the intellect and the spiritual moments and have a nice day. Now, back to your regularly scheduled show."

Would that give you enough permission to realize that you are doing life just as you are supposed to? The bottom line is, there is no "how to get out of it," because it's what we do. We continually drop in and out of depths of understanding. After all, how exciting would life be if we were all just enlightened without the bruises of our humanness to give it a touch of color?

Going back to the idea that, according to statistics,

I will live to be 78 years old, I have decided to reject the status quo and I'm going to live longer than that stupid statistic. I will have a book-signing party when that day comes! And, when the day arrives, I'm sure I'll do some intellectual thinking about the Three Principles on my deathbed. By that time, my biggest worry will be peeing in the bedpan.

*To judge another is based on ego; to see another is based on wisdom.*

Elsie Spittle

# — Question #5 —

## Why do people resist the simplicity of the Three Principles?
## In other words, why doesn't this make sense to everyone?

I love it when new people join me at the recovery center. Usually, they aren't coming to the center to hear my words of wisdom. A lot of times, they have already been to treatment of one kind or another, and hearing something again for the hundredth time doesn't excite them.

There was a new guy who came into the center. He'd been in and out of rehab for years. He can recite the 12 Steps in his sleep. I like this guy. He's got jet-black hair, slicked back with every piece combed as if lined up to go to work. He comes in with his arms crossed most of the time, and with a stern look on his face, ready to dismantle whatever the team leader has to offer. Behind the austere appearance, you can tell that he still wants to figure life out, and even though he comes in acting like he's got it all down, there's a part of him that wants to discover something new.

I was teaching the Principles the best way I could, and he stopped me midsentence when I was talking about the inside-out nature of life and its simplicity.

He told me, "Amir, let me get this straight…you are saying that you can see something new out of nowhere and somehow, magically, your life can be all rainbows and unicorns?"

The group laughed and I knew that this could either be a disaster or a teaching moment for both of us. So I went to what I know. I always go back to the source of where our experience is coming from. I looked at Mike (don't worry, that's not his real name; I would never share his real name…Bob would get mad if I did) and asked him a few questions.

"Mike, have you ever been sober?"

"Yeah, I've been sober. I used for 10 years and sobered up for two years."

"OK, good. What stopped you from using after 10 years?"

"What do you mean? I went to a 12-step program that I didn't want to go to and just sat there while the guy was blabbing about something."

"OK, then what happened?"

"I decided to learn the 12 Steps, and I became sober, that's what happened."

"Step back for a minute. What happened before you learned the 12 Steps?"

"I was in the room telling myself that this is stupid, but I'll give it a shot."

"Give what a shot?"

"I'll give this 12-step thing a shot."

"When you gave something a 'shot' what happened

for you to do that?"

"I had a change of heart. I thought it would be interesting."

"Did you hear what you just said?"

"Yeah, I heard it, I just said it. I thought it would be interesting, I said."

"Yes…you had *a thought!* You had *a thought* that showed up and .0005 seconds before that thought you were an addict for 10 years of your life. After the 'I'll give it a shot' thought, you became sober for two years. Before you decided to give the 12 Steps a try, you had to have a thought. You had to have a thought to say, 'Maybe I'll try this.' The thought that appeared allowed you to take the next steps! **You had a thought!"**

He sat there for a minute, then said, "Shit, you're kinda right. I guess I was looking at all the things after that, that appeared to get me sober. It was a lot of work, but having that thought wasn't work at all. But if that thought hadn't appeared, I wouldn't have seen the next steps toward my recovery."

### One Thought Changes Everything!
(Somebody should write a book with that title!
What do you think, Mara Gleason?)

The reason we miss the simplicity of the Principles is that it's subtle, silent, and fast. By the time the thought comes through, the actions preceding it have taken the forefront. We give credit to the action; however, a change of heart needs to occur in order for any action to make sense. A change of heart is simply a new thought.

It happened so fast that Mike missed the fact that it all came down to his capacity for *new thought*. When you go back to the starting point, you can see that something shifted first, and this shift happened in thought without his consent or permission. In other words, you don't have the right or say to have a new thought come through...because it doesn't come from you! Where it comes from is up for debate. Just enjoy the fact that you can see something you didn't see for 10 years suddenly show up out of nowhere! It's easily missed because we think we're in control of what we see. We think it takes will or might for something to look different.

The truth is, clarity shows up on its own. It happens so fast that once you see the clarity, you forget what brought that clarity. We get an insight and we go off and running on a new venture; we have a new way of seeing the world. Or we get bogged down in thought, we misunderstand it, and blame the circumstance. Just go back to the source and you will see where it's coming from.

The resistance isn't directed at the Three Principles; the resistance is simply a misunderstanding of their source, which comes back to the Three Principles. When a client, a parent, a child, or whoever, can see where the source originates, nobody will argue or believe it doesn't make sense. And even if they don't think it makes sense, simply ask them what about it doesn't make sense, and bring them back to the source. If it's a feeling, there will always be a thought behind it. If it's a thought, there will always be a feeling behind it.

When we give a person the chance to see it for themselves, how could they possibly *not* see it? It's most likely because we have taken the Three Principles and made them complicated. We start getting theoretical and it becomes a debate.

Folks, this is an understanding! This is true for everyone. Make it simple, ask them what they see and where it comes from, and they will have no choice but to see it for themselves.

All roads lead to these Three Principles. Whatever people are experiencing is happening with the Principles of Thought, Mind, and Consciousness. If the person you are speaking to doesn't agree, they have to use the Principles to disagree. That's to our advantage. Take them back to see that — or better yet, let the person you are speaking to take *themselves* back to these three Universal Truths. You might be speaking to someone who was an addict for 10 years, and found that the start of their sobriety came from a single thought or change of heart. As a Zen master once told his student, "Opening one's eyes may take a lifetime. Seeing is done in a flash."

*The only trick in life is to be grateful for your highs and graceful with your lows.*

George Pransky

# — Question #6 —

## I've had insights. I get the Three Principles. So...why do I feel like shit? I know it's just thought!

*I know nothing about it all and see no difference between you and me. My life is a succession of events, just like yours. Only I am detached and see the passing show as a passing show, while you stick to things and move along with them.*
Sri Nisargadatta Maharaj, *I Am That*

I'm going to flip the question inside out and see if this makes sense to you. "I've studied fevers. I understand how fevers work, so why do I feel like shit? I know it's just my body fighting infection!"

Listen, if you knew how fevers worked you wouldn't ask the question. When you have a fever, your temperature rises, you feel sluggish, and you probably need to rest. That's actually how fevers work. If they didn't work that way, then a fever isn't fevering™. (I'm trademarking that word!)

If your thoughts didn't give you the spectrum of experience, from feeling like shit to absolute bliss, then a thought wouldn't be thoughting™. (I'm trademarking that one too!)

The Principles are simply telling you that you will experience the energy of Thought in the moment, moment by moment by moment. What you will experience is what "thought" leaves at your doorstep.

The good and bad news...

Thought will give you an experience of bliss and it will also give you the illusion of despair. The important part for me isn't why I feel how I do; it's to know that the energy of Thought must be working if I feel anything.

The other option is to be dead. When you are dead, you won't feel like shit. But you also won't feel happy, insecure, excited, hurt, jealous, curious, resentful, grateful, or whatever feeling you can imagine. You'd need to be alive for those. You'd also need the energy of Thought to give you the spectrum of emotions.

Sorry folks, if you are alive, the bundle comes with all of the emotions and feelings. It's an all-inclusive package. So, be grateful you have a package that allows you to see the colors of life!

*Concentrate on yourself. ... Whatever you are, is all you can give away. That's very simple. You open your wallet, you have a dollar: That's all you can give away. You open your mind and it's full of anger, hate and distrust, sadness: That's all you can give away. But if your mind's full of love, that's what you can give.*

Syd Banks

# — Question #7 —

## When should I start sharing and what qualifies me to share? How much grounding do I need?

*I have four great vows:*
*When I'm hungry, I eat;*
*when it's cold, I put on more clothes;*
*when I'm tired, I stretch out and sleep;*
*when it gets warm, I like to find a cool breeze.*
Baiyun Shouduan

I volunteer at a recovery center. I am not a therapist, I am not a counselor, and I have never abused drugs. Every week I go to the center to speak about what occurs to me to speak about in the moment. How is that possible?

Let's go back to the beginning, when one of my friends came over to discuss my process for writing books.

"Amir, how have you written five books and I am not able to get a single page out of my head?"

I chuckled. "I never wrote a *book*. That sounds scary to me. I wrote a *sentence*. After I wrote a sentence, it became a paragraph. After a paragraph, it started to look like a chapter. If you told me I needed to write a chapter by the end of the week, I wouldn't know what to do with it."

Of course, that was how I saw it in that moment. When I would do it the "scary" way, writing a book was miserable. What's the "scary way" of writing a book? I would create an arbitrary, heavy burden on myself called "WRITING THE BOOK." Then I would give myself an arbitrary, make-believe timeline. If I didn't cross the invisible finish line at the time I made up, I felt like a failure. When I used to do that, WRITING THE BOOK seemed to be daunting.

Luckily, I discovered early on that if I am going to make stuff up, I should probably remember that I made it up. So I was giving myself multiple jobs.

1) WRITE A BOOK!
2) Manage all the thinking around WRITING A BOOK
3) Reduce the stress of time management that I made up
4) Manage feeling like a failure for sitting in front of a computer with all this thinking around my book instead of writing the damn thing!

Then, I came to my senses and found out what my job entailed. My only job is to start jamming on a computer and let the end result speak for itself.

I'm not sure what he heard in that conversation, but it wasn't about my writing process. He saw the role thought played in his procrastination. He realized that the book wasn't the problem. It wasn't the problem at all. He had to battle the *idea* of writing a book before he could sit down and even type a single word.

He started to ask me questions about how I handle certain clients I work with. He got curious about what grounding means, how it applies to working with clients, and what "tools" I use to work with them.

I wasn't qualified to speak like a therapist, I was only qualified to speak like me. He saw something beyond my qualifications. We are working with people, not theoretical models! In my experience, the first point of contact should be from our place of humanity. That is something I can bring to the table.

Out of the blue, he asked me if I'd be willing to share "whatever just happened to me" with his clients at the recovery center. I couldn't have planned that. If I told you that I'd be working at a recovery center because I spoke to one of the therapists from the center about writing a book, you wouldn't have believed me. I wouldn't be qualified to share such a miracle. Luckily, qualifications weren't needed; a connection and conversation toward truth were needed. This doesn't mean qualifications for certain jobs aren't necessary; it means that when we are speaking about the Three Principles or what we see, all that is needed is for us to show up and see what we see. It's a different space of knowing and seeing.

Let's get back to you. I don't know what qualifies

you to share the Three Principles. What qualifications were enough for you to pick up this book? What qualifications did I have in order to have permission to enter your world and offer you my thoughts? Look, those questions would be valid if qualifications were part of the requirement to share. However, we are not in a court of law and we are not trying to get to an end result.

I tell my coaching clients that when you are in discussion with a client, it should be more like you are visiting a museum. When you visit a museum, both of you are curious, excited, and waiting to see something you haven't seen. We aren't working from a place of *qualifications*, we are working from a place of *exploration*.

How much grounding do you need to go to the museum? Even if you are in a low mood, you're apt to see something. When we get bogged down with qualifications, grounding, knowing, and all this stuff that comes from our intellect, we forget one thing... **that we made it up!**

When we forget that we made it up, we think there is a unique thing that qualifies us to share. The good news is, *you* are the unique thing and you can share at any point of your journey. If that doesn't satisfy you, I'll give you a checklist of requirements you must acquire to share the Three Principles.

To be qualified to teach the Three Principles you MUST:

- Be born in Scotland
- Live most of your life in British Columbia
- Have a ninth-grade education
- Be a welder
- Have a temper at times and tell people to relax and go home and stop thinking so much.

Oh wait, that's Syd Banks. I forgot that his qualifications would have been the laughing stock of all qualifications. But he wasn't in the qualifications game. He was in the Truth game. He wasn't interested in seeing whose ideas would withstand a word battle, he wanted to point to something that's true for all of us, beyond the words. He was adamant that people knew that he wasn't qualified to speak about anything except for what he knew. Matter of fact, if you read his book *The Enlightened Gardener*, the gardener, Andy, who spoke about these Principles, would continually tell the qualified psychologists, "Are you sure you want me to try to explain my idea?" He said, "After all, I'm untrained in your field and I don't want to cause any ill feelings because of different opinions."

He knew that if he got into an ideology battle, nobody would win. Nobody would hear anything besides their own point of view. He wasn't interested in that at all. You shouldn't be, either.

That's the good news with the Three Principles.

We are sharing what we see to the best of our ability. That is comforting to me. That is good news to me. That means we can all share, we can all learn, and we can all explore.

We are not looking to win a fight, see who's right, or use our might! (You see what I did there?)

As long as we point toward the direction of truth, we will see something. That's all the qualification I need. How about you?

*All you have to know is everything is created from thought, you don't have to know anything else.*

Syd Banks

# — Question #8 —

## Do all the questions answer themselves and just dissolve when you get a better/different/deeper grounding?

had to take a break from writing this book at one point, so I went outside for a moment and walked around my back yard to get a breath of fresh air. As I was walking, I noticed a huge spider next to a plant. I didn't think we had bugs that big in San Diego. As any grown man would do, I shrieked and proceeded to walk away to collect myself. When I returned to look at the spider, I noticed he hadn't moved one bit. Upon closer examination, I noticed that it was actually a piece of bark that looked like the scariest bug I had ever seen. I laughed out loud and went back inside to answer this next question.

Do all questions answer themselves and just dissolve when we get a better/different/deeper grounding?

Let's define *grounding* first. *Grounding* to me means a direct relation to how reality is created moment by moment. When we see where reality is created, it gives us a better navigation tool. The source of all reality goes back to the Principles of Thought.

PERIOD! My questions about what I needed to do with the bug disappeared because I wasn't dealing with a real bug. What ended up happening was the questions changed when my experience correlated to what I was experiencing.

As I see it, the questions don't necessarily dissolve, it's that the questions don't mean the same thing when we see things from a different space. The different space is when we see where our reality is coming from. If we think our job is causing us stress, or traffic is giving us anxiety, we will create questions to relieve the circumstance. If you think you are dealing with an Amazonian spider in your back yard, when in fact you had an illusionary experience, you will create questions to resolve your thinking around your circumstance.

The answers dissolve because we have the gift to visualize what we can't see via insight. We have the capacity for wisdom to come through and show us "bark spiders" or "bark thoughts"; thoughts that appear to be real and urgent until we get a glimpse of where they are really coming from. That doesn't mean that we aren't going to have circumstances that are not going to appear hard, tragic, or helpless; it means that when we are face-to-face with a circumstance, we have an infinite possibility and capacity to see it; however, reality shows up for us at that moment.

For any circumstance that we face, we are not obligated to see the world the way we saw it one thought ago. That gives us true freedom to see the question change, dissolve, resolve, or disappear at a moment's glance.

The good news is, you don't have to do anything to dissolve it. The "it" that dissolves happens because we have the capacity to see something new at any moment. That was built into the software when we were born.

*If we can forgive everyone, regardless of what he or she may have done, we nourish the soul and allow our whole being to feel good. To hold a grudge against anyone is like carrying the devil on your shoulders. It is our willingness to forgive and forget that casts away such a burden and brings light into our hearts, freeing us from many ill feelings against our fellow human beings.*

Syd Banks

# — Question #9 —

## How do we stop ourselves from getting caught up in other people's stories and not getting defensive?

When we ask questions like this, we are looking at it backwards. It is too late to give you a proper answer. That's like going back to the story in question #8 and asking, "What do you do when you get caught up thinking you just saw a huge spider, when in reality it was made of bark?"

I do what I do based on what I just saw. I jump and freak out! What else can I do? In the same respect, if you get caught up in other people's stories you are, well…caught up! That's what we do when we get caught up; we get caught up! And when we get caught up, we get defensive! And when we think we saw a huge spider (made of bark or made of spider stuff) we jump!

I looked up "getting caught up" to see what it means. Getting caught up means that you were sidetracked or taken away from what you originally set out to do or planned. And we generally plan to be level-headed. And getting sidetracked simply means we forgot where our experience is coming from. We think that our feelings are coming from other people's stories. If that's where we think our feelings are coming from, then why wouldn't you get defensive?

Once the mind clears, we start to see that the story is just that — a story. The feelings and the color of the circumstance need to come alive through thought. And as we get caught up in the special effects of the story, we feel it come alive. That's what the Principle of Thought is supposed to do!

By the time we arrive at the behavior part of the situation, it's too late in the game. We are going to navigate the best we can until we see something new. The part that's important to know is:

**YOU WILL ALWAYS SEE SOMETHING NEW!**

You will always see something different. You were designed to experience a new reality once the old thought passes.

To answer your question, we can't stop ourselves. However, there is no need to do so. In the same way I can't stop myself from seeing spiders made of bark until I see them, there is no way to stop you from seeing thought take form in the moment and giving the circumstance life until you see it's made of bark...I mean thought.

Go out there and get caught up! Join the drama, get excited, get mad, freak out!

Rumi had a good way of looking at getting caught up. He said:

This being human is a guest house. Every morning a new arrival. A joy, a depression, a meanness, some momentary awareness comes as an unexpected visitor. Welcome and entertain them all. Even if they're a crowd of sorrows, who violently sweep your house empty of its furniture, still treat each guest honorably. He may be clearing you out of some new delight. The dark thought, the shame, the malice, meet them at the door laughing, and invite them in. Be grateful for whoever comes, because each has been sent as a guide from beyond.

I would add a bit to that and say that the crowd of sorrows will soon look different when we know that wisdom is always available. Momentary awareness shows up as the unexpected visitor and brings with it gifts to wake us up from Thought. Sometimes I need the unexpected visitor to remind me and nudge me to wake me up from where I am. That's a good thing. In other words, if we see the guests as visitors and not intruders, we can welcome them in. We can utilize their gifts to steer us back to Truth. And the Truth is, all those guests are thought-generated. They join you when you wake up every morning. What a gift! This allows me to get mad, hurt, and get caught up in other people's stories. Knowing the Principles, and knowing that a new thought will give this moment of reality new life, allows me to be OK in the uneasiness that life appears to bring. Something about this being true is useful for me.

*You don't look out there for God, something in the sky, you look in you.*

Alan Watts

# — Question #10 —

## How do we know what our gut is telling us?

My gut makes all kinds of noises! If it's hungry, it makes alien noises. When it's full, my gut pops out and tells the world I've overeaten. My gut also tells a lot about my health. I am guessing you're not asking me literally what my gut is telling me. When this question is posed, we want to know something that is intuitive, beyond logic, and insightful for us.

Our body and soul have spontaneous ways of working with life. When we use our fight-or-flight response, we call that **in**stinct. When we get a spontaneous answer beyond what we can 'think,' it's called **in**tuition. Notice that both words start with "**in**." That's important. It means that it comes from within you.

How do we know what our gut or intuition is telling us? From my experience, intuition has a different feel. It's a knowing. It doesn't feel accumulated, like knowledge. It's new, fresh, and hits you from out of nowhere.

We can follow the direction in which we are going based on what we experience.

As Syd Banks said in *The Missing Link*, "As our consciousness descends, we lose our feelings of love and understanding, and experience a world of emptiness, bewilderment and despair. As our consciousness ascends, we regain purity of *Thought* and, in turn, regain our feelings of love and understanding."

There is a different feeling when we see something for ourselves. There is an easiness to it, a softness that we feel inside. I've sensed it in myself and I've seen it in others. It's a calmness that appears in the midst of the lack of clarity.

I'm doing the best I can to explain how I feel when I get a gut feeling. I know you've had gut feelings. How did you know when you got one? Where did that feeling point you to? Did the gut feeling come with a thought? Continue exploring this question and you'll get better at noticing the feeling of wisdom coming through you.

*All we are is peace, love, and wisdom, and the power to create the illusion that we are not.*

Jack Pransky

# PAGE 62
# IS
# AMAZING!

**Inside joke alert!**

(Go to page 102 to get in on the joke!)

# — Question #11 —

## Why do some negative or unhelpful thought patterns repeat themselves over and over in my head?

*As you think, so you shall hear.*
*The sage hears fools and wise alike.*
*The fool hears only fools.*
*The Missing Link* by Syd Banks (page 85)

When we are in negative or unhelpful thought patterns, we get caught up in them. They feel real. They color the world we see. Things don't start going our way, which further confirms that the thoughts we are having must be how reality is showing up.

When we, as the thinker, can see the energy of Thought flow and go up and down, we can see its usefulness. When we are having negative thoughts or misled thoughts, it's uncomfortable. We know that in this space, it's hard to find peace. We try to resolve this unease by asking more questions, which leads us away from the wisdom we seek.

Why do I feel this way?

Why can't I stop having negative thoughts?

When is this going to go away?

Why does this always happen to me?

And so on.

As Syd says, the fool hears only fools. When we are stuck in thought, we become foolish. We continue with the questions that keep us in a low mood. We continue to search in the space of low feelings and contaminated thinking. We wonder why it won't go away while we sit in the space of negative thought. But! When we glance beyond personal thought and see its nature, we become sages. We see the negative and positive as energy in the moment. Getting a glimpse is enough for me to not dive in and wonder about the where, what, and why of the energy of Thought taking form in this moment.

Zen master Sengcan once said, "The great way is not difficult if you just don't pick and choose." That's what we do. We concern ourselves when we get a negative thought and hope to get somewhere else.

This I know to be true:

1) I will have a negative thought.
2) I may or may not engage in thought taking form.
3) No matter how often it repeats itself, something new always shows up.
4) It's not my job to fix the energy of thought when it shows up.
5) If I force questions with the same feeling I want to get away from, I get stuck in more negative thought.

6) You will get out of whatever current thought you are in because the system is designed to give you new thought.

7) You are designed to have low moods and high moods. As psychologist George Pransky once said, "The only trick in life is to be grateful for your highs and graceful with your lows."

8) If it's part of the human design, then there isn't a problem with having patterns repeating themselves. The problem is when we see the *repetition* itself as the problem. The problem further expands when we "think" we should be somewhere else besides where we are in this moment.

Imagine if I flipped the question inside out: Why do some **positive** or **helpful** thought patterns repeat themselves over and over in our heads? What would you tell that person? You wouldn't have much to say. You'd say, "Go on, then! Why are you asking me such a silly question?"

We see that having positive thoughts or helpful thoughts is normal. We see that it's part of the design to have a string of positive thoughts show up in Thought. So, why does having a string of negative thoughts seem so foreign?

When I realized that the system was designed to give us both, the question became less relevant. It's when I start to give it an arbitrary amount of time before I "should" be back into a positive state of mind that I experience more grief.

It's when I say something like this to myself: "OK, I know it's just thought. I know I'm feeling the energy of thought in the moment, but it's been 8 minutes and 34 seconds already! I need to meet the new boss, and this feeling is going to screw it up! I'm giving you 2 more minutes or else…or else I am going to feel worse!"

It doesn't work that way. However, when you are stuck in unhelpful thoughts, just knowing that it is thought can make a tremendous difference, wherever you may be.

Let's imagine for a moment that you had only one channel on your radio and you are enjoying listening to this station. All of a sudden, a Justin Bieber song comes up, and you hate Justin Bieber! What would you do? Would you go around asking why the station sometimes plays songs you don't like? No, if you know the nature of radio stations, you'd know that you're only one song away from hearing something new. Songs always change; it's the nature of radio playlists. Now, if you didn't know that, I could see why it would be bothersome. Even worse, what if they had a Justin Bieber marathon? You'd have to listen to more than a few songs! Again, if you know that eventually even Justin is going to run out of songs, that wouldn't be a problem either.

There is nothing in the rulebook that states you

can't garden, go to work, kiss your kids, read a book, meditate, ride a bike, write a book, or whatever, while Justin Bieber is playing in the background.

There is also nothing in the rules that states you can't garden, go to work, kiss your kids, read a book, meditate, ride a bike, write a book, or whatever, while the energy of Thought is playing in the background.

The important part isn't whether we are stuck in thought; it's knowing that the system is designed to get mucked up from time to time. The system is also designed to self-regulate. So, let the system do what it does. You just go on and do the life part, regardless of what thought happens to appear in this moment. A new song is bound to come along.

*You can have your experience without your experience having you.*

Linda Pransky

# — Question #12 —

## What about the biochemical theory of depression and anxiety — how does this relate to the Three Principles?

*"Is there any difference between what you were talking about and cognitive therapy, Andy?" Janet asked.*

*"I really don't have an idea what cognitive therapists believe or don't believe," he answered. "I'm no therapist, Luv. I only know what I know, and what I am saying doesn't apply to you four because you are therapists. What I am saying pertains to every human being in the world."*

Syd Banks, *The Enlightened Gardener*
(pages 50-51)

This is a tough one. I am not a scientist or a doctor, so I will tell you what I know from my personal experience. I'm going to circumnavigate the question because I want you to see the brilliance of our wisdom in action, despite having a hormonal deficiency and having all the biochemical markers to show that I was a poster boy for anxiety, depression, and suicidal ideation.

Do you remember the first story I shared, about the doctor who told me I was pretty much screwed from taking the hair-loss pill Finasteride? In short, Finasteride is what's known as a 5-alpha-reductase Inhibitor, also known as 5AR-I. The idea behind the drug is that it reduces or removes DHT from the body. High DHT levels in men is correlated with male pattern baldness. The bad news is, DHT is also the male hormone that produces the libido, erection, muscle growth, and all the sexual function you need.

For the 5AR-I enzymes to work, they basically have to destroy the communication bridge to all the other hormones in our system. Bottom line, this stuff messed me up bad. It wasn't "in my head." I could prove to you I was messed up by my bloodwork, scans, spinal fluid...you name it.

I wanted to share that bit because I was living proof that biochemically and hormonally I was a mess. But despite that mess, I was able to see this wisdom that we all have, no matter what biochemical issues arose.

So, grab a cup of tea and I'll tell you a story. I promise this will answer the original question. If it doesn't, I hope you liked your tea.

After having my crash from taking Finasteride, I began experiencing unusual thoughts. Killing myself came to mind more than usual, and for some reason, those thoughts didn't bother me. Maybe it was because I knew what they were made of. Who knows? But I was having thoughts about not living anymore, not seeing a purpose in life, and it was happening all too often. There was also an emotional numbness I'd never experienced before. It was like somebody had hit the off button on the emotional spectrum. The master volume for all emotions was near zero. Imagine watching a car crash and people dying, and you experience it the same way as taking out the trash. That's what I was feeling. Even with the emotional numbness, I'd get crazy thoughts I'd never had before. My brain was going haywire, and the one thing that "popped" me out of what was happening was when I went to visit my mom.

My mom made her typical Persian dish of rice and seasoned meat, and we ate and chatted like we always do. Then she looked at me and asked if I wanted seconds.

My body shifted as if I'd heard her say that I was the least-loved child in the family. For a moment, I envisioned taking a pen I'd seen (it was a blue pen with a cap on it) and jabbing her neck with it.

I noticed that her asking me this and me having a reactionary thought like that didn't make sense....like, absolutely no sense at all! I was blessed. The thought was so vile and uncalled for, that I could, with 100% certainty, know that this was thought-generated.

The thought was too crazy for me to believe. I knew something was up. I needed that! That got me to realize that whatever I did, in my chemical brain, shit was going haywire. But it was OK; I needed a crazy thought like that to know that it wasn't normal to want to jab my mom in the neck with a pen.

Now, why do I think that's wisdom? Because I needed a thought like that to remind me of where my experience was coming from. Surely, my mom asking me for seconds wouldn't justify me wanting to jab her with a pen, let alone a blue one.

I'm just glad the thought wasn't about how much of a lowlife I was. I might have believed that one. Or that I was broken. I might have believed that one too. Or all the other "little" meaningless thoughts that can feel more legit and easy to believe.

In my craziness, my wisdom pulled through to show me what I needed to see. The thought needed to be a crazy, outlandish, "What the fuck are you thinking?" kind of a thought.

When thoughts like that showed up again, I was ready and waiting. I knew they would come again with full force. And they did. The crazier they got, the more I was able to see where they were coming from. So, I wasn't afraid of them. In truth, I started to enjoy them.

This is why I see the importance of what Syd shared. This is where it makes all the difference, to be able to see life for what it truly is. If I didn't know what was happening, I would have believed I was done and broken. After all, take a look at my bloodwork. I didn't have hormones regulating. I didn't have bio-chemical markers telling me I was "normal." Shit, I was even having thoughts that I was crazy. But I also had one thing that you can't take away from anyone, no matter their physical limitations — their access to spiritual strength, resiliency, and wisdom. I still had that! I got to see it for myself. I was still free!

Yes, biochemical and hormonal deficiencies can change or blur reality. But you still need to use the same principles to experience whatever reality you are seeing. You are also equipped with wisdom that shows up at the most opportune times to allow you to see beyond what you see at the moment.

I was blessed. I got to see the craziness of what Thought can bring to the table. I also had enough in me to see the illusory nature of what was showing up.

I was blessed to know a little about how thought plays a HUGE role in experiencing life. (*Huge* is an understatement — Thought is the main player!)

Now, does that mean I didn't go back to the doctor to fix my biochemical and hormonal issues? Of course, I went back! Why wouldn't I repair the physical issues that might be messing with the software?

In the meantime, whatever my biochemical markers are telling me, I still have the ability to see past my physical make-up and go to the spiritual self that can see beyond what is in front of me.

If you have a biochemical issue or hormonal issue, see a doctor! Get it fixed the same way you'd fix a tire. You can still get from point A to point B on flat tires, but it just might be an easier ride if all your tires are filled with the right amount of air. The same thing applies here. You can still live life, but it's nice to know that you're running on all cylinders...at least in the physical world.

And regardless of what's been messed up biochemically or hormonally, you have access to wisdom, innate health, and love. You also have the ability to see where the essence of thought originates from. In my experience, I was gifted access to see the deeper truth of that in spite of my hormonal mess of a mind.

It has become more irrelevant to see how my life fits in with the Principles. Instead, I see how the Principles are always present in life, no matter what is happening biochemically, hormonally, physically, emotionally, etc. There always seems to be room for wisdom to shine through. Always!

As long as the Principles of Mind, Consciousness, and Thought are working as one, wisdom from a deeper place is available, even if the hardware breaks down. It's good to know that I'm always going to be OK.

*When you are already 'home'...you don't have to take an Uber to get back.*

Amir Karkouti

# — Question #13 —

# I am an NLP Practitioner and I have discovered the Principles! Now what? Should I continue doing NLP (or any other modality) or stop?

I will try to answer this question as objectively as possible, but I'm not sure whether I will be able to. After all, I am an NLP Master Practitioner — or at least, I used to be. So, I'll do my best!

I remember asking Michael Neill the NLP question a long time ago. I said, "Surely all those years of NLP must have been the reason you got here."

His answer, if I recall, was, "Had I discovered the Principles earlier, I would have probably saved myself 10 years of training."

This is the important bit for me...**DISCOVERING.**

As you go through your journey, you will see more and more. You will have further glimpses as you look in the direction of discovery. You will DISCOVER more as you see for yourself.

The answers will show up as you go on your journey. Don't worry about what anyone "thinks" you should do.

I had just finished writing a book called *The Happiness Formula* when I discovered the Principles, and I didn't know what to do once it got published. It was an NLP book with tons of strategies and neat tricks that could be used to ease the mind. But after I wrote the book, I saw things differently — I saw something *new* — and couldn't even believe the things I had written.

You know the first thing I did?

I laughed!

For a long time!

Just a few minutes before I saw something new, I thought the book was the best thing that had come out of my mouth...until it wasn't anymore.

So, I laughed!

Looking back, I did all the things I did from what I could see in the moment...and so will you.

Instead of wondering whether you should continue with NLP or other modalities, see if it makes sense for you, at this moment, to continue. If it does, go for it. If there is a bit of doubt, see where that doubt is coming from and explore that too.

You can't make wrong turns. You can only gain lessons, so enjoy the ride!

The quote below sums up all the turmoil and questions I had when I was going through the Three Principles (3P) Transition.

..I would like to beg you dear Sir, as well as I can, to have patience with everything unresolved in your heart and to try to love the questions themselves as if they were locked rooms or books written in a very foreign language. Don't search for the answers, which could not be given to you now, because you would not be able to live them. And the point is to live everything. Live the questions now. Perhaps then, someday far in the future, you will gradually, without even noticing it, live your way into the answer.

(Rainer Maria Rilke, 1903, in *Letters to a Young Poet*)

Or, as Ram Dass so eloquently put it, "The next message you need is right where you are."

So, don't listen to what I'm saying, listen to that voice inside you. It will tell you something sooner or later, better than anything I could say.

*The Three Principles is not a self-improvement course, trying to improve what is. Rather, it is understanding the nature of what is.*

Dicken Bettinger

# — Question #14 —

## I know the Principles and I can't get myself to go to the gym! What's wrong with me? How can I get inspired?

*When you are free of the world, you can do something about it. As long as you are a prisoner of it, you are helpless to change it. On the contrary, whatever you do will aggravate the situation.*
Sri Nisargadatta Maharaj

I f only the Three Principles would magically give me enough motivation to force me to go to the gym. However, the Principles aren't there to motivate you; they are simply a description of how both life and reality work.

And life sometimes gives us 101 reasons why we shouldn't want to go to the gym today. It will also give us a host of other useful and not so useful ideas and thoughts.

The good news is, motivation is not a necessity for going to the gym. I used to think it was. I relied heavily on my state of mind to make decisions. Whether it was getting up in front of a crowd of 200 people to speak about the Three Principles or getting myself ready to walk into the gym, I used to think that a certain thought was necessary to give me clarity or a kick start into a healthier, better body.

I found something out after going to the gym when I was inspired, tired, angry, frustrated, mentally hurt, curious, psychologically frustrated...you name it. I found out that my state of mind has nothing to do with me being able to lift weights.

So now, I go to the gym and bring my annoying chatter with me. The good news is, I can lift weights, regardless of the chatter.

This is the most strategic I will get in this book. Notice that there have not been any prescriptions presented in this book thus far. However, if you want to go to the gym, yet you have a mental block...are you ready for this?

## GO TO THE GYM ANYWAY!

And if you have negative thoughts about going to the gym, or have no motivation, then I would highly suggest that you...

## STILL GO TO THE GYM!

There is no way around this one.

And like my 18-month-old baby has shown me, she does not care whether it's raining or sunny outside. She is outside playing as if it's her last day on Earth. That was a cool lesson for me. She intrinsically figured out that, rain or shine, she can play.

I have realized from watching my daughter that I can go to the gym, despite my foggy thoughts, and I can play with whatever decides to show up in my head.

I don't have a good Principle answer for you for this one. Well, actually, I do…

Are you ready to hear it?

## SHUT UP AND DO THE WORK!

Let Universal Mind sort out the noise in your head! Your biceps will thank you for it!

(This is also relevant for writing a book, creating a seminar, planning a trip, or starting a business!)

*Good morning, this is God. I will be handling all your problems today.*

God

# — Question #15 —

## How do you prepare to speak to different audiences about the Three Principles?

This is a great question. Do you speak differently to doctors than you would somebody in a recovery center? Would you speak to engineers differently than a group of artists? How should someone prepare for different genders, occupations, groups, lifestyles, etc. when sharing the Three Principles?

I live in San Diego, one of the best places on Earth. I can ride my bike to the beach and get ice cream whenever I want. Imagine if I parked my bike and I saw somebody drowning. Imagine that, while they were drowning, I stared at them from shore, asking myself, "I wonder if I should call myself a lifeguard, a good swimmer, or a Good Samaritan before I jump into the water?" Do you think that the person drowning really cares what I call myself? He's probably wondering what the hell I'm doing talking to myself instead of jumping into the water to help him!

I used to "prepare" my talks as if their job title mattered. I used to strategize about how I was going to make the biggest impact, whether the person or group in front of me had more money than me or not.

After sharing the Three Principles with enough people, I realized something:

WHO THEY ARE DOESN'T MATTER.
WHAT THEY USE TO CREATE LIFE DOES!

Everyone I have worked with uses Universal Mind, Consciousness, and Thought to create the reality they are experiencing. Everyone I have worked with has the ability to see beyond what they are seeing at this moment. Everyone, no matter how rich or poor, how smart or ignorant, has the right to experience the spiritual gifts of this teaching.

But we screw it up. We put our arbitrary labels on how we should introduce the Principles.

"Oh, Bob is an atheist. Don't talk about it as a spiritual thing. Bob gets really mad and you've never seen Bob mad! Tell him the Three Principles are based on chemistry."

"Janet! Oh, Jan made $50,000 more than me this year. Surely, she doesn't have the same ups and downs via thought that I do. I need to wear a nice watch and have an expensive PowerPoint presentation to sell her on the Principles!"

Folks, it's a disservice to bring your judgments into something that could change someone else's world. The good thing everyone has going for them is that before they were an accountant, a doctor, a soldier, a drug addict, a nurse, a priest, a mom, a rapper, or whatever...they were and still are...A HUMAN!

That's the best thing we have going for us with sharing the Principles — that we are dealing with humans! Actually, that's the *second* best thing going for us. The *first* best thing is that we are telling the truth about how life works. We are ahead of the game. But we screw it up! We screw it up because we let titles, gender, history, or whatever, get in the way of sharing this truth.

The two things to remember before doing any groups, talks, or coaching, are:

1) You are sharing a universal fact about how life works via Mind, Consciousness, and Thought.

2) You have humans in front of you who need to hear it, no matter what occupation or social class they come from.

## That's it!

Just share what you know. Share from your experience. Share from the truth of what you have seen. From that place, you will forget who you think you should be, and the person listening will remember who they really are.

*We did not all come over on the same ship,*
*but we are all in the same boat.*

Bernard Baruch

# — Question #16 —

## What happens when I've been around the Principles for years, but I no longer get anything new or have insights, and I'm not even sure I understand the 3P's anymore?

*Information is just bits of data.*
*Knowledge is putting them together.*
*Wisdom is transcending them.*
Ram Dass

When I was younger, I was afraid to fly. It wasn't actually the flying bit that scared me, it was when the plane would ascend into the air. I remember reading somewhere that the most dangerous part of a flight is when it departs and lands. I'm not sure whether that's true, but regardless, I embraced that thought and decided to believe it with full force. Not a great idea if you like traveling.

I remember sitting there and strapping on my seatbelt. I was shaking. I looked around and wondered why nobody else cared. I tried reading. I closed the window shade so I didn't have to see outside. Nothing helped.

The next thing I knew, the pilot got on the intercom and said, "Good afternoon, passengers. This is your captain speaking. First, I'd like to welcome everyone on Flight 405. We are currently cruising at an altitude of 33,000 feet at an airspeed of 400 miles per hour. The time is 1:25 p.m. The weather looks good, and with the tailwind on our side, we are expecting to land in San Diego approximately 15 minutes ahead of schedule..."

As the pilot continued his speech, the seatbelt light turned off and I realized something. While I was concerning myself with the make-believe scenarios of my life on this plane, the plane went up 33,000 feet without me noticing. I could have literally walked back and forth on the plane and wondered when this stupid plane was going to level off...while all the while it was already leveling off.

Discovering the Three Principles has felt the same way for me. After my initial "holy effin' God" moment, I settled down and waited for the next "holy effin' God" moment...and it didn't come. I was wondering if I was "doing" the Principles wrong. I wasn't. It's just that I was at a higher level of under-standing. What I did notice was that my life was simply easier, more relaxed, and even more enjoyable for the most part. However, I wasn't getting the BIG insights, like when I had first heard the Principles, so I almost dismissed the beauty of my life along the way.

My fatherly advice is this: Sit your ass down, look

out the window, and enjoy the ride. You'll be cruising at infinite depths of awareness in no time. You'll see what you see during various depths of consciousness. Granted, the insights might not look or feel the same as when you first heard the Principles; however, if you obsess over why the insights aren't BIG anymore, you might miss a chance at a new, more subtle insight. Even worse, if you are pacing around the aisle waiting for something to happen, you'll miss all the gifts that life has to offer. So, sit back, grab a coffee, and look out the window of life. You might just find something you didn't see before.

As I'm writing this, I'm questioning whether I even completely understand the Principles anymore myself. I go in and out of being able to articulate it. In one way, it feels distressing; in another way, it's comforting. It might be because I'm *living* the Principles now. Maybe that's my next "level" of understanding. Maybe the next "level" is for me to *live* them rather than *articulate* them.

Regardless, it's not my job to figure out whether I can wrangle with the intellect (although it's fun to do at times). My job is to get back to life and let life give me the insights I need when I need them. And if I don't "get" anything new like I used to, maybe that's exactly where I need to be right now, at this moment. When I look at it from that vantage point, that seems awfully new to me! And something about that is comforting.

*Our plans never turn out as tasty as reality.*

Ram Dass

# — Question #17 —

## How do I share the Principles with others?

I was at a bachelor's party a few years back, and was in charge of planning excursions for the weekend. Well, I *thought* I was in charge. When you have a group of 20 drunk men together, planning is not really a part of the plan.

I had breakfast scheduled for the next day and a trip to ride four-wheelers. My plans were disrupted when more than half of the group didn't make it to breakfast. Most of them were hung over and didn't even know what day it was.

I vented my frustration to one of my friends. I think he channeled Syd or something. He said to me, "Don't worry about planning to have fun. The only thing needed for this group to have fun is our tight friendship. The rest will sort itself out."

I'm not sure why I heard something in that. Immediately, I dropped all the other plans and just had fun with everyone. I stopped trying to plan the unplannable.

I'm not saying that sharing the Principles is like planning excursions with a bunch of drunk guys on holiday, but I am going to tell you that you can't plan what shows up. I share the Principles the same way I plan my connections with friends. I just show up.

Here is what I *don't* do when my friends show up, because it would just be weird:

Friendship rules:

1) Greet them and make a sarcastic remark.
2) Tell three jokes, then make a crack at their mom.
3) Ask a serious question so they know I am a real friend.
4) Go out to lunch and buy them a drink.
5) Ask them what they are up to and if they want to hang out soon.

Now, this is stuff that may or may not happen, but if I brought a piece of paper and checklisted everything above, that would have ruined the "friendship" or the essence of friendship.

However, we do that "checklisting" thingy with the Principles. I've had people say things like:

1) Should I have a PowerPoint presentation?
2) Is it important to talk about Mind, Consciousness, and Thought?
3) How many metaphors should I use in the conversation?
4) Do they need to listen to a Syd Banks audio before my session?
5) I've done 10 trainings so far; do I need to do 45 more before I share this stuff, even though wisdom is already equipped in us?

# Whoa, now...SLOW DOWN!

You don't have to do any of that unless you want to! **You cannot plan what you haven't experienced yet!** So chill out. Let the conversation steer you.

Here are a few things to keep in mind to help you better navigate:

1) Everyone has an innate capacity to see beyond personal thinking.

2) Everyone is bound to get an insight into something, whether you did a good job or not.

3) Having an exploratory conversation will put both people on an equal playing field.

4) Don't worry about doing it right. Be present *right now.*

5) If you aren't present, you can tell the person that you aren't present. Tell them what is happening in real time. This will also give them a glimpse of how mind/thought works.

6) Take a wrong turn; you'll eventually find your way back home.

7) None of the answers will be on the test. You and the other person already have all the right answers. The cheat sheet is inside of you already.

8) Teach what you understand. Teach only from what you know. At that point, you don't have to be an expert. You just need to tell people what you've seen.

The more you share, the more you learn about the Principles. You start to see that your state of mind matters less and less as you share what you know. The sharing itself brings you a better understanding of the Principles. You get to see in real time that your state of mind changes as you think about sharing this stuff. Regardless of your state of mind, you can connect to a deeper wisdom inside of you. The more you share, the less you care where your state of mind is. You can create the content by seeing the fluctuation of thought, which is changing this very moment.

Syd Banks would say, "As you share, you learn." Keep sharing, get yourself out into the world, and you will get a deeper understanding of these Three Principles. If you are at a loss for words...that's always a great place to start too.

Here is another trick that I've found useful. Go out and do a shitty job! Just go out and tell people what you see. It may come out as gobbledygook, but just tell your friend you're insane and that you want to share your insanity.

I'm writing this right now and I feel like some of it is shit. I'm good with that. I'm not concerned at all. Let it be shit. Wisdom hides in mysterious places. I have truth by my side, even though you may or may not see where I'm pointing. Sometimes you'll be brilliant, and sometimes you'll have nothing amazing to say. If you want to share this stuff, just keep talking. Don't worry about being brilliant. As Jerry Hyde wrote in his book, *Play from Your F*&King Heart*, "Don't be brilliant 'cos to attempt to create a great piece of work is the shortest route to mediocrity that I know."

And as you start to care less and less about how to share it, what will be left is what's in your heart. And what's in your heart is what the other person has been yearning to hear all their life. Go out and share it the best way you know how. Yes, there will be bumps in the road in sharing what you can see. Like the astronauts said during their trip back to Earth in Apollo 13, "You never know what events are going to transpire to get you home."

You are never that far off from where you are pointing to. Just keep sharing. The more you share, the more you learn. There is no shortcut.

And if it's still a struggle to share the Three Principles, give them this book! After they read it, they will be so confused that you will sound like a genius.

*There's nothing you need to do, be, have, get, change, practice, or learn in order to be happy, loving and whole.*

Michael Neill

## — FINAL QUESTION —

## I have found my innate health.
## What now?

The answer is on the next page...

# GO LIVE!

*Mental life is a story. Real life is a divine transformation.*

Dr. Vijai S. Shankar

I hate endings! I miss all of you already. Thank you for reading and please send any love letters, hate mail, questions, or thoughts to amir@amirkarkouti.com

If you want to continue the conversation and you're not sick of me yet, please check out the *What The F*#$ Are The Principles* Facebook Group. Visit **www.welovesyd.com** to join!

**Please read the next page.
It's really important!**

# IMPORTANT! PLEASE READ!

DEAR READER,

I have a favor to ask of you. I am not looking to be a bestseller. I am not striving to have this be the definitive book on the Three Principles. Some people do a much better job describing these three gifts of life than I do. What I do want to bring to the table is light-heartedness around the 3P's. Sometimes, spiritual ideas can get bogged down and feel "heavy." I didn't want that to happen with this book. I hope there was enough wisdom mixed with humor to have you reach this final chapter.

Here's what I am asking of you: I would love it if you would write me a review on Amazon.

## Before you write a review...
## STOP AND READ BELOW!

Because this book is all about bringing more lightheartedness to a subject that can otherwise feel a bit heavy, let's keep that spirit going in our reviews!

How do we do that, you ask? Oh, you are going to love this!

Write whatever you like in your review and THEN, somewhere in the review, make sure you write some version of this: *"...and whether you read the whole book or not, you HAVE to check out page 62! **Page 62 is AMAZING!"***

I want people to go to Amazon, read the reviews, and literally say, "What the hell is this book about and what's on page 62?"

I want this to be fun, erratic, and something that's never been done before!

**The more you talk about the book and PAGE 62, the more cosmic points you will receive!**

After you have written a review, let me know and I'll send you something special. It will be my gift to you! You can email me at amir@amirkarkouti.com after you post a review.

Thanks for taking the time out of your precious life to join me on this ride.

With love,
Amir Karkouti

# ACKNOWLEDGMENTS

I want to give a quick shout-out to all the people who helped come up with the questions for this book. I created a Facebook Group called *What the F\*#K Are the Principles* and asked many of my beloved members their most pressing Three Principles questions. To my surprise (actually, I'm not too surprised), I had an incredible response and some intriguing questions. Thank you to everyone for giving me the context for this book.

Here are the names of all the people who jumped in and gave me questions to reflect on. I can't thank you enough for playing with me. This book would not have been created without the people listed below. You all inspired me to get this book out into the world and you gave me a lot to think about. For that, I am truly grateful!

Steven Heath
Robin Lockhart
Mary Schiller
Dorren Boonzaier
Ryan Simbai Jenkins
Karl Walkinshaw
Pete Bailey
Brooke Wheeldon-Reece
Ellen Stoune
Satyajit Joel Peters

Imogen Caterer
Robert Block
Elizabeth Lovius
Nick Bottini
Jill Whalen
Judy Nahkies
Theodore Hamish Tomlinson
Jeff Radar
Ivan Nikolaev Dimitrov
Piers Thurston
Marlena Tillhon-Haslam
Lindsey Reed
Vijayraj Kamat
Melinda "Lindy" Greenacre

A BIG Thank you to all my teachers and colleagues who continue to open my eyes to this beautiful truth.

To my "angels" in the recovery center, who have allowed me to see further into the Principles than I thought possible.

To my clients, who have explored this space with me and trust me as their guide to the unknown.

To Cris Wanzer, my editor, who sliced, diced, and chopped up this book so you don't have to figure out what the hell I'm trying to say! She is literally the other half of this book! I am so grateful for an editor who understands my way of thinking and who helps me put my thoughts onto a blank sheet of paper. You can find her at: www.ManuscriptsToGo.com

Finally, to my wife, who thinks I have no idea what I'm talking about 90% of the time, but still loves me.

# Who Was Sydney Banks?

Sydney Banks (January 25, 1931 – May 25, 2009) was a welder with a ninth-grade education who had a life-changing insight revealed to him. The revelation he discovered was that all of life is experienced by the Three Universal Principles of Mind, Consciousness, and Thought. He believed that these Three Principles would be the gateway to everyone's psychological freedom. For over 40 years, these Principles have made their way into hospitals, sports psychology, recovery centers, education, correctional facilities, social services, corporations, and people's lives, all over the world.

The biggest gift he shared is that anyone can attain spiritual freedom and access to infinite wisdom. His simple writings and offerings have helped end mental suffering for millions of people worldwide.

Mr. Banks, although I never met you, I wanted to say thank you from the bottom of my heart for letting me see the gifts that were hidden inside of me. Although your physical body is not here on this Earth, your spirit continues to spread light to many of us, each and every day. Thank you for being an ordinary mystic and for letting so many of us see the magic and mystic in ourselves.

Sydney Banks passed away at his Salt Spring Island home in 2009.

# Who Is Amir Karkouti?

Do I really have to write this? It's very weird to have to write about myself, but I will for the sake of the book.

Hi, my name is Amir Karkouti. My name is also on the front of the book. I own a chain of restaurants in San Diego, speak to amazing men and women about our Innate Health at West Coast Recovery Center in Carlsbad, and I work with groups and one-on-one to share the Three Principles in a practical and sometimes nonsensical way. Before you think this is an intro to my online dating profile, let me also tell you that I am married to my soul mate. I also have a beautiful daughter, Aria, who reminds me that a big part of living is to dance and play. I hope Aria and I remember to play and dance for the rest of our lives.

Addicted to the
Principles?

We Can
Help!

What the F*#k Are The Principles
Institute for Living

# FINAL NOTE!

IF YOU KNOW ANYONE WHO IS ADDICTED TO
THE PRINCIPLES, PLEASE SHARE THIS
INFORMATION WITH THEM!

Did you discover the Principles only to find yourself constantly looking for answers?

Are you like many in the community who are looking for another hit of "insights," good feelings, and better states of mind?

YOU ARE NOT ALONE!
We can HELP.

At the What the F**K Are the Principles Life Institute, we work directly with people like you who have been consumed with learning about the Principles and are forgetting to live.

Does this sound like you?

- You have a question about the Principles, get an answer, and realize it's not satisfying enough.
- As soon as you have a rough day, you try to convince yourself it's all thought and beat yourself up for not seeing it.
- Do you have the urge to tell others about the Principles to a point that friends and family believe you've lost control of life? (Don't

worry, we alleviate this.)

- Are you burying yourself in seminars, books, and audio programs so you can feel how it felt when you first got the blast of freedom from discovering these Principles?
- Do you jump from forum to forum, asking the same questions in hopes of satisfying your analytical mind?
- Do you notice that when you get an answer, you respond immediately with, "I get that, but what about this?"
- Do you write article after article or post quotes in hopes of feeling that you are helping others, only to satisfy your own ego? (I've been there and I know how that feels.)

## WELL, YOU'RE NOT ALONE!

At the What the F**K Are the Principles Life Institute, we take these issues seriously and we have worked with thousands of people from the 3P community to get them back to their lives.

At the What the F**K Are the Principles Life Institute, you will learn how to:

- Have a bad day, and, well…have a bad day! No trying to fix it, no Syd tapes, and no need to read *Relationship Handbook* for the fifth time…(of course, unless you want to).
- Meet with friends and not wait for them to have

a problem so you can jump in and save their lives. Yes, you will be able to listen to people and not have to give advice, a teaching, or a recommendation unless they ask you. You will have the freedom to listen and empathize and leave it at that! (We have a special home for people addicted to this behavior. Please visit our waterfront location.)

- Stop trying to come up with new analogies, new ways to "explain" the unexplainable, and just start talking to others from a human level. You will have the freedom to mess up, not know what you're talking about, and not worry that it's not good enough if asked what the hell you're talking about.

AND FINALLY...

At the Life Institute, we will take you outside to coffee shops, retail stores, and beaches, to show you that 99% of other creatures and mammals live just fine not ruminating about the Principles all day.

I know, you found the Principles to find freedom and now you are shackled by the thing that gave you the freedom in the first place.

It doesn't have to be that way!
We can help!

Call us Today 1-800-Back2-Life or visit the *What The F\*#K Are the Principles Facebook Group.*
Counselors are standing by...

**Remember...the Solution is Seeing that there was never a Problem in the First Place.**

# RESOURCES STRAIGHT FROM THE HORSE'S MOUTH

## Books, Audio Recordings, and Videos by Sydney Banks

**Books**:

*In Quest of the Pearl*
*Dear Liza*
*Island of Dreams*
*Second Chance*
*Enlightened Gardener*
*Enlightened Gardener Revisited*
*The Missing Link; Reflections on Philosophy and Spirit*

**Audio Recordings:**

*The Great Spirit: Reflections on North American Native Spirituality*
*Attitude! Dealing with Stress and Insecurity*
*Hawaii Lectures*
*In Quest of the Pearl*
*Long Beach Lectures*
*One Thought Away*
*Second Chance*
*Washington Lectures*
*What is Truth*

**Videos**:

*Hawaii Lectures #1: Secret of the Mind*
*Hawaii Lectures #2: Oneness of Life*
*Hawaii Lectures #3: Power of Thought*
*Hawaii Lectures #4: Going Home*
*Long Beach Lectures #1: The Great Illusion*
*Long Beach Lectures #2: The Truth Lies Within*
*Long Beach Lectures #3: The Experience*
*Long Beach Lectures #4: Jumping the Boundaries of Time*
*Washington Lectures #1: The Three Principles*
*Washington Lectures #2: Separate Realities*

Made in the USA
Middletown, DE
30 June 2021